"THIS DESIRABLE COTTAGE..."

A Farce in One Act

by

ANTHONY BOOTH

SAMUEL   FRENCH

LONDON
NEW YORK TORONTO SYDNEY HOLLYWOOD

Copyright © 1960 by Samuel French Ltd
All Rights Reserved

THIS DESIRABLE COTTAGE is fully protected under the copyright laws of the British Commonwealth, including Canada, the United States of America, and all other countries of the Copyright Union. All rights, including professional and amateur stage productions, recitation, lecturing, public reading, motion picture, radio broadcasting, television and the rights of translation into foreign languages are strictly reserved.

ISBN 978-0-573-02271-5

www.samuelfrench.co.uk
www.samuelfrench.com

For Amateur Production Enquiries

United Kingdom and World excluding North America

plays@SamuelFrench-London.co.uk
020 7255 4302/01

Each title is subject to availability from Samuel French, depending upon country of performance.

CAUTION: Professional and amateur producers are hereby warned that THIS DESIRABLE COTTAGE is subject to a licensing fee. Publication of this play does not imply availability for performance. Both amateurs and professionals considering a production are strongly advised to apply to the appropriate agent before starting rehearsals, advertising, or booking a theatre. A licensing fee must be paid whether the title is presented for charity or gain and whether or not admission is charged.

The professional rights in this play are controlled by Samuel French Ltd, 52 Fitzroy Street, London, W1T 5JR.

No one shall make any changes in this title for the purpose of production. No part of this book may be reproduced, stored in a retrieval system, or transmitted in any form, by any means, now known or yet to be invented, including mechanical, electronic, photocopying, recording, videotaping, or otherwise, without the prior written permission of the publisher. No one shall upload this title, or part of this title, to any social media websites.

The right of Anthony Booth to be identified as author of this work has been asserted in accordance with Section 77 of the Copyright, Designs and Patents Act 1988.

CHARACTERS

(In order of appearance)

BILL BLAGSHAWE
JULIE, his wife
DON ANDERSON
SALLY, his wife
WOODY
ZINA
FRED

The action of the Play takes place in the living room of the cottage by the sea called "Chez Nous"

Time-the Present

"THIS DESIRABLE COTTAGE..."

SCENE—*The living-room of a cottage by the sea called "Chez Nous". There are french windows C back which give on to the garden. There is a door leading to the kitchen R and a door down L leads to the bedroom. A small table stands down RC with two wheel-back chairs R and L of it; there is a settee LC and L of this is a small easy chair. R of the french windows is a Dutch dresser (dressing only).*

When the CURTAIN *rises the room is empty. After a moment* BILL *and* JULIE BLAGSHAWE, *a young couple, arrive outside the french windows.* JULIE *peeps in.*

JULIE. Oh, darling, isn't it a dream. Come on.
BILL. Wait, this is a very important occasion. Ready?

(BILL *puts the bags down and lifts* JULIE *up, carrying her downstage* C)

JULIE. Oh, darling. (*She takes off his hat and tosses it on to the settee*)

(*There is a shower of confetti. They kiss*)

Mmn . . . put me down, darling.

(BILL *does so*)

(*She moves* L *turning in an excited circle*) Oh, isn't this wonderful. Our little world for a whole fortnight, just you and me —Mr and Mrs Blagshawe. You know I can still hardly believe it. But it's true, look. (*She pulls off her glove and shows her wedding ring*)

(BILL *laughs and moves* R *to half sit on the table.* JULIE *sits on the settee*)

BILL. Do you remember what the fellow said at the reception? "Don't forget to take a tin of brasso with you in case the ring turns green." Damn cheek.
JULIE (*innocently*) I didn't quite understand that.
BILL (*cheerfully*) Well, you see, when a bloke takes a girl

away for a week-end he usually gives her a brass wedding ring and—well—er . . .
JULIE. Yes.
BILL (*lamely*) Well—if you don't clean it, it turns green (*He laughs a little falsely*)

(JULIE *gets up and goes to him*)

JULIE. You seem to know an awful lot about it, Bill.
BILL. Me?
JULIE (*suspiciously*) Yes. That came rather pat. You haven't at any time—er . . . ?
BILL. Of course not, darling. Why?
JULIE. Well, I don't know, you are a man of the world, I mean you've been abroad, you went on that day trip to Boulogne last year.
BILL (*taking her in his arms*) You are not starting our married life with doubts, are you?
JULIE. Of course not, darling.

(BILL *kisses her tenderly*)

Oh, Bill.
BILL. Better now?
JULIE. Mmn. You couldn't do *anything* wrong in my eyes, darling. (*She breaks from him a little*) Come on, let's explore the place.
BILL. I'll get the bags.

(JULIE *goes off* R. BILL *collects the bags from the window and then comes down* C.
JULIE *comes in again*)

JULIE. This is the kitchen.
BILL (*nodding* L) This must be the bedroom then. (*He puts his hat on his head and starts to move* L)
JULIE. Wait a minute, I'll take the picnic bag. (*She takes it from him and pulls out a small bottle of milk which she puts on the table. She looks at it proudly*) There, how's that for organization? Now we can have our first cup of tea.
BILL. I don't think I feel like any.
JULIE. Oh, we must have some after that awful train journey. Put the bags away and I'll have a scout round.
BILL. Right.

(JULIE *takes the picnic bag and goes out* R, *pausing at the door to blow him a kiss.*)
BILL *does the same then goes out* L.
After a few seconds JULIE *comes back excitedly and calls him*)
JULIE. Come on, Bill.
BILL (*emerging*) You haven't made it already.
JULIE (*coming to him and taking his hands*) No, I want to show you something. There is a wonderful little garden at the back simply bursting with ripe blackberries. Let's pick some.
BILL (*aghast*) What, now!
JULIE. Yes, why not?

(BILL *sits at the* L *end of the settee and yawns rather obviously*)

BILL. Well, I was feeling rather tired.
JULIE. But, darling, it's only nine o'clock.
BILL. Yes, I know, but it's been a very hectic day.

(JULIE *sits* R *of him, spins round and lies back with her head in his lap*)

JULIE. But this is fun, I bet no-one else has picked blackberries on their wedding night.
BILL (*grimly*) I bet they haven't either.
JULIE. I'm dying to make you a pie tomorrow.
BILL. Aren't you a funny mixture. You spend three weeks choosing a going-away outfit which costs the earth and which no-one else will ever copy, and then in the same breath you risk ruining it by blackberrying in it. Let's do it tomorrow.

(JULIE *sits up and cuddles him*)

JULIE. No, Bill, we've got to do it now, I've got a sort of thing about it. I feel that if we don't, something awful will happen. Do you ever get those sort of feelings?
BILL (*firmly*) No.
JULIE (*wheedling*) I know it sounds awfully silly, but—please, Bill.
BILL (*sighing*) Oh, well, if you feel that way about it.
JULIE. I do, really.
BILL. All right. (*He gives her a quick peck*)

(*They get up to go*)

(*He suddenly stops her*) I think we'd better change into old clothes or something. (*He brightens visibly*) I've got a wonderful idea. Let's change into our pyjamas and dressing-gowns, pick the blackberries and then we shall be already for bed.

JULIE (*quickly*) No, I don't think so, Bill.

BILL. Why not?

JULIE (*shyly*) Well, I'm not a prude or anything, but I think there is something vaguely indecent about blackberrying in a shortie nightie.

BILL. Oh.

JULIE. I know, I've got a plastic mac in the picnic bag. I can slip that on and it doesn't matter how dirty it gets. Ready?

BILL (*sighing*) Yes.

JULIE (*moving towards the door down* R) Isn't this fun?

BILL (*raising his eyes*) Marvellous.

(JULIE *leads* BILL *out* R.

There is a pause then DON *and* SALLY ANDERSON *appear outside the french windows. They are a young couple*)

DON. This looks like the place, hold on and I'll check. (*He looks at the name-plate above the window*) That's it. *Chezze Noose*.

SALLY. That's a funny name for a cottage.

DON. Well, it's plain enough. C-H-E-Z-Z N-O-U-S. *Chezze Noose*. (*He stands back and rubs his hands together*) And now, Mrs Anderson, *if* you please.

SALLY. Oh, Don, this is so romantic.

(DON *tries to lift her but fails*)

DON. It would be easier if you put the bag down.

SALLY. Oh, yes. (*She puts her case down*)

(DON *tries again*)

Are you sure you can manage, darling?

DON (*gritting his teeth*) Of course.

(DON *struggles in with* SALLY, *trips and they both fall in a heap downstage* C)

SALLY (*anxiously*) Are you all right, darling?

DON (*hopping around*) Oh, it's nothing, just a broken leg. Never mind about me, are you all right? (*He goes on his knees beside her*)

SALLY (*miserably*) I've laddered my stocking.
DON (*grandly*) What's a stocking, I'll buy you a new pair tomorrow, I'll buy a dozen pairs.
SALLY (*happily*) Oh, darling.

(*They embrace and kiss*)

DON. What are we kneeling down here for, let's get comfortable. (*He gets up pulling her after him. He starts to act as if he is doing an old-time melodrama*) Come, woman, at last I've got you in me power.
SALLY (*acting*) Nay, sir, nay.

(DON *stands on the settee dragging* SALLY *towards it*)

DON. Come, woman, thy fate is sealed.
SALLY. Have mercy, sir, I am but an innocent maid.
DON. Ha ha!
SALLY. Let me go or I shall scream.
DON. No-one will hear you, this old mill is far from town.
SALLY. But, sir . . .
DON. You protest too late—come. (*He gives a violent heave. Her glove comes off and he disappears from sight over the back of the settee*)

(SALLY *rushes to it and peers over*)

SALLY. Don! Darling, are you all right?

(DON *appears slowly above the settee and hands Sally her glove*)

DON. Up till now, this hasn't been my night, has it?
SALLY. You are not hurt, are you?
DON. Nothing that really matters. Come on, let's get settled in. (*He collects the bags from the window and takes them down* L *and puts them by the bedroom door*)

(SALLY *lies full length on the settee with her head at the* R *end of it*)

SALLY. Oh, this is wonderful. No noise and above all, no people. Fourteen days of uninterrupted bliss, and I don't care if it rains every day.

(DON *goes to the back of the settee and looks down at her*)

DON. Happy?

SALLY. Delirious.
DON. Do you realize we have been married five whole hours.
SALLY (*sighing*) Five hours.
DON. No regrets?
SALLY. None. We'll be the happiest couple in the world. There will be no quarrels in *our* life, we'll show people what marriage really should be.
DON. That's what I like to hear. (*He leans over and kisses Sally then moves to the window and looks out*) Gosh, this is a wonderful view, worth that awful train journey down. Weren't those other people awful? I hope we . . .
SALLY (*seductively*) Don—come and spoil me.

(DON *grins, comes down and sits on the edge of the settee and kisses her*)

Mmn . . . that was nice.

(DON *gets up and moves to the door* L)

DON. Well, I suppose we had better find our way around. I wonder what this is. (*He opens the door*) Ah yes, this is the bedroom. I wonder what that one is over there?
SALLY. I expect it's the . . .
DON. No, that's the little shed at the bottom of the garden.
SALLY. Well, it must be the kitchen then.
DON. That's an idea. What about a cup of tea?
SALLY. Oh, darling, I didn't bring anything.
DON. What are we supposed to eat then?
SALLY (*swinging into a sitting position*) I thought I'd slip out first thing tomorrow morning and get some stores from the village.
DON (*resigned*) It's Sunday tomorrow.
SALLY. Oh, I forgot that.
DON (*getting annoyed*) Blimey, that's a fine start. I thought you said you'd got everything organized.
SALLY (*peevishly*) Sorry, but I didn't think of food.
DON (*getting more angry*) Well, you should have.
SALLY (*angrily*) Well, if it comes to that, you should have reminded me.
DON (*almost shouting*) The kitchen is your department,

not mine. If I have to think of everything throughout our life things are going to be . . .

(SALLY *gives a loud wail and bursts into tears*)

(*Frightened he goes on his knees and takes her in his arms*) Oh, darling.

SALLY (*sobbing*) Our first quarrel.

DON. Never mind, darling, I was just being selfish, I'm sorry.

SALLY. No, it was my fault, I should have remembered . . .

(DON *dabs her eyes with his handkerchief*)

DON. Let's forget it. I tell you what, have a look in the kitchen, there might be something there and I'll get the bags into the bedroom.

SALLY. All right.

(SALLY *goes out* R *rather miserably.*
DON *takes the bags out* L.
They both return almost at the same moment)

DON. Any luck?

SALLY. Not a thing, only crockery. (*She sees the milk bottle on the table*) Oh, look, there is a bottle of milk. Now isn't that kind of Mr Rosenberg, he knew we would have trouble getting some at this hour and remembered to leave a bottle.

DON (*crossing to her*) Oh, well, it's better than nothing.

SALLY. I'll get some cups.

(SALLY *goes out* R *and returns at once with two cups.* DON *pours half a cup each. They link arms continental fashion*)

DON. To us.

(*They drink*)

SALLY. That's better.

DON. Fancy starting a honeymoon on milk.

SALLY. I love it.

DON. Very fattening.

SALLY. I don't care.

DON (*lightly*) Don't care was made to care.

SALLY (*seductively*) When you put it that way it sounds different.

(*They kiss*)
I'll wash these up.
Don. Can't it wait till the morning?
Sally. I'll put them in the kitchen, anyway.
Don. All right.

(Sally *takes them out* R. Don *wanders over to the* L *arm of the settee and sits on it.*
Sally *appears a few seconds later*)

Sally (*shyly*) Well, I suppose we had better start unpacking.
Don. Not a bad idea.

(Sally *crosses to the door* L)

(*He goes on one knee*) Shall I carry you across?
Sally. If it's all the same to you, I'll walk.
Don (*grinning*) Windy.

(Don *and* Sally *go out* L. *There is a brief pause.*
Then Bill *appears* R, *sucking his thumb, he sits at the* L *end of the settee.*
A very worried Julie *trails after him*)

Julie (*anxiously*) Darling, are you all right?
Bill. It will stop bleeding in a minute. I've never seen thorns like those.
Julie. I'll get some water to bathe it.
Bill. No, no, it will stop—in time.
Julie. But it might be poisoned.
Bill. I'll risk it.

(Julie *kneels on the settee beside him*)

Julie. Well, we'd better not pick any more.
Bill (*quickly*) Oh, no, that would be courting trouble.

(Julie *gives Bill a little kiss on the forehead*)

Julie. You poor darling. Now you just lie there and I'll make you a nice cup of tea.
Bill. Lovely idea.

(Julie *moves to the table and stops dead when she sees the bottle half empty*)

Julie. That's funny.

BILL. What?
JULIE. Most of it has gone.
BILL. Tripe, it can't have.
JULIE. Well, look for yourself.

(BILL *glances casually in her direction*)

BILL. Well, what do you know!
JULIE (*accusingly*) You pinched it.
BILL. Me? How could I, I was with you all the time.
JULIE. You went back to the kitchen for a couple of minutes.
BILL. Only to get some paper for the bottom of the basket.
JULIE. Yes, and while you were there you hogged the milk as well.
BILL. But I never came in here.
JULIE. Now look, Bill, I'm not a child, milk doesn't disappear into thin air, there isn't anyone else for miles around.
BILL. But I keep telling you . . .

(JULIE *stands there adamant with her arms folded*)

JULIE. Your mother was quite right, she said, "Watch him, he's a milk swigger."

(BILL *gets up and faces her*)

BILL. I beg your pardon?
JULIE. You swig milk from bottles and woof all the cream, leaving the blue watery stuff for other people.
BILL. My mother said that?
JULIE. Yes, she said she'd never been able to break you of the habit. Do you deny it?
BILL. Well, not exactly, but—well, you must admit it's hard to resist. An icy cold bottle, loads of cream on the top . . .
JULIE (*quietly*) Darling, I'm not blaming you. Everyone has a weakness somewhere, yours just happens to be milk, only I didn't think you'd start quite so soon.
BILL (*grimly*) I never touched that particular bottle.
JULIE (*sighing*) Oh, really, Bill.
BILL (*angrily*) I tell you I never laid a finger on it.
JULIE (*coldly*) There is no need to shout. I've told you, I don't mind. What does upset me is that you bother to deny it.

BILL (*furious*) I tell you . . .

JULIE (*getting angry*) I mean, if you are going to lie about little things now, what is it going to be like later on when serious issues arise?

BILL. But, Julie . . .

(JULIE *storms furiously to* R *and faces him*)

JULIE. It's a fine start to our married life . . . I mean after only six hours. What will it be like in six years?

(BILL *goes over to her, speaking very quietly*)

BILL. Will you do me a favour?
JULIE (*coldly*) Certainly.
BILL. Go and make some tea.
JULIE (*archly*) Very well.

(JULIE *starts to go out* R. BILL *raises his hand as if to spank her, but she suddenly turns round at the door for a final rejoinder. He smoothes his hair instead*)

You'd better come with me, otherwise we shan't have any milk at all.

(JULIE *and* BILL *go out* R.

After a moment DON *appears* L. *He calls to Sally in the bedroom*)

DON. Sure you don't want any more?
SALLY (*off*) Positive.
DON. Then I think I'll finish it. I'm parched.

(DON *goes to the bottle and drinks the remainder. He puts the empty bottle down and goes out* L *again.*

After a pause JULIE *bustles in* R)

JULIE (*coldly*) Will you put the kettle on?
BILL (*off*) Yes.

(JULIE *goes to the* L *side of the table picks up the milk bottle, then puts it down rather quickly, putting her hand to her mouth*)

JULIE (*tremulously*) Bill?
BILL. Yes?
JULIE. Darling—come in here.

(BILL *appears* R)

BILL. What's the trouble now?

JULIE (*pointing*) Look, it's empty.
BILL. Well, that's a fine thing. You do the very thing you tick me off for.
JULIE. But, darling, I haven't touched it.
BILL (*airily*) A likely tale.
JULIE (*coming down to him and taking his arm*) Bill sweet, you must believe me. It was empty when I came in.
BILL (*suspiciously*) Let's have a look at your mouth. (*He inspects her mouth*) Well . . .
JULIE. Oh, Bill, I'm frightened, there is something funny here.
BILL. Perhaps the bottle leaks.
JULIE. Oh, don't be silly, it's as dry as a bone underneath.
BILL (*slowly*) That's true.
JULIE. Perhaps the place is haunted.
BILL (*laughing*) Oh, tripe.

(DON *drops something heavy in the bedroom. They both look startled and* JULIE *flies into* BILL's *arms*)

JULIE. Oh, darling, I'm scared.
BILL (*doubtfully*) There is nothing to be scared about. I expect it is someone playing a practical joke. I'll just get that lump of wood we found at the bottom of the garden.

(BILL *strides out* R. JULIE *finds herself alone*)

JULIE (*shrieking*) Darling, don't leave me.

(JULIE *rushes out after him.*
After a moment SALLY *appears* L, *dragging a reluctant* DON *towards the window*)

SALLY. Come on, just as far as the sea and back, it won't take more than a few minutes.
DON (*sighing*) Oh, very well, only why we have to take a walk at this time of night beats me.
SALLY. It's so romantic. There is a heavenly moon and besides it will make us sleepy.
DON. Well, who wants to be sleepy?
SALLY (*coyly*) Oh, Don, you say the most awful things. Come on.
DON. Oh blast, I've forgotten my cigarettes. You wander on and I'll catch you up.

(DON *goes back into the bedroom* L.
SALLY *wanders out of the french windows.*
After a moment a very timid JULIE *appears* R. *She is armed with a large wooden spoon. She goes to the window and peeps out, then comes down behind the settee to the* L *end of it and bends down to see if anyone could be underneath it.*
At this moment DON *enters* L. *With a broad grin he scoops her in his arms with a loud cry of triumph*)

DON. Ha ha! Once aboard the lugger and the girl is mine.

(JULIE *kicks furiously.*
At this moment BILL *enters* R *with a large piece of wood*)

BILL (*angrily*) What the hell do you think you are doing?
DON. Who are you?
BILL. What are you doing with my wife?
DON. Your what! (*He looks at Julie for the first time*) Oh blimey! (*He drops her in a heap on the floor*)
BILL. Well, what have you got to say?
DON (*floundering*) Well, I thought—well, I don't know what to say, you see . . .
BILL (*coldly to Julie*) Perhaps you can explain.
JULIE. Explain what?
BILL. What you were doing in his arms, being carried off in *there*. (*He indicates the bedroom* L *with his stick*)
JULIE. Bill, how dare you!
BILL. It all fits now, you get your secret boy friend down here thinking that I . . . No wonder you didn't want to turn in. Well, it's a good thing I found out in time, isn't it?

(JULIE, *furious, scrambles to her feet*)

JULIE. You think that I . . . With a total stranger . . . Oh, this is the end. I've never been so insulted in my life.
BILL. That's right, try and brazen it out.
JULIE. Brazen it out! Ooh . . . (*To Don*) Well, don't just stand there, hit him for me.
DON (*weakly*) But I don't even know him.
JULIE (*wildly*) Well, that doesn't stop you, does it?
DON. Now wait a minute for crying out loud. In the first place, who are you and what are you doing here?

"THIS DESIRABLE COTTAGE . . ." 13

BILL. You mean you don't know her?
DON. I've never seen her before.
BILL. Well, what were you doing with her in your arms?
DON. I thought she was my wife.
BILL. Don't you know your own wife?
DON. She is wearing the same clothes and I didn't give it a second thought, besides I only saw her backsi . . . er from behind.
JULIE. How can your wife be wearing the same outfit? This is a model, there isn't another one like it.
DON. That's what *you* think.

(SALLY *appears at the window*)

SALLY. Aren't you ever coming, darling? Hullo, who are these people?

(*There is a horrified silence as* SALLY *comes down to* JULIE'S *level and they both glare at one another. Their dresses are identical*)

BILL. How much did you pay for that *exclusive outfit?*
JULIE (*furious*) Oh, shut up.
DON. Well, we'd better get this sorted out. Who are you for a start?
BILL. I'm Bill Blagshawe.
JULIE. And I'm Julie Adams and we've taken this place for a fortnight.
DON. Oh, it's that sort of set up, is it?
JULIE. What do you mean?
SALLY. Well, we *are* married. (*She crosses and takes Don's arm*)
JULIE. So are we. (*She moves quickly to Bill and takes his arm*)
DON. But you said your name was Adams.
JULIE. I meant to say Blagshawe.
DON. I'm sure you did.
BILL. You needn't say it in that tone of voice. We were married this afternoon.

(DON *looks meaningly at Sally*)

Look if you don't believe me, I've got my marriage lines here. (*He moves to Don then stops*) What the hell am I doing? Why should I show them to you anyway.

Don. I don't know, but you were doing all the insisting.

Bill (*putting the wood on the table*) If it comes to that, who are you and what are you doing here?

Don. Well, I'm Don Anderson and this is my wife Sally and we've taken this cottage for the next two weeks for our honeymoon.

Julie. You must have mistaken the dates. You must be the following fortnight.

Sally. Oh, no, we've got the dates right, the twelfth to the twenty-sixth.

Julie. But those are our dates.

Don (*moving over to them*) I'll show you my agreement—there you are in black and white.

Julie. Where's ours, Bill?

Bill (*producing it*) There you are, you can't have it plainer than that, the twelfth to the twenty-sixth.

Don. But this is ridiculous, what are we going to do?

Bill. I suppose you couldn't take the following fortnight?

Sally. We can't wait a fortnight.

(*They all look at her*)

I mean it's not practical, we can't get a month off from our jobs.

Don. In any case, why should we? Damn it all, this is our honeymoon.

Julie. And it's ours, too.

Bill. Well, this is a fine how do you do, I must say.

Julie. It's very obvious that there has been a double booking. If the worst comes to the worst I suppose we could share the cottage. I mean, it has two rooms—we could move one bed into the kitchen.

Sally (*coldly*) There *is* only one bed.

Bill. That's helpful.

(*There is a pause while they think*)

Don (*cheerfully*) Well, of course, we could always . . .

Julie (*firmly*) Oh, no, we couldn't.

Don. You don't even know what I was going to suggest.

Julie. I can guess.

Sally (*quickly*) Don't you talk to my husband like that.

Julie. I will if I want to.

(*The two girls face each other angrily*)

SALLY. Well, I like that, you have the darn sauce, a complete stranger in our cottage . . .
JULIE (*firmly*) Ours.
SALLY. To stand there and insinuate that my husband . . .
BILL (*testily*) Oh, shut up, this is getting us nowhere.
DON. Did you tell my wife to shut up?
BILL (*irritably*) Yes, I did.

(DON *marches over to Bill and swings him round*)

DON. I've a damn good mind to punch you on the hooter.
SALLY. That's telling him, Don.

(JULIE *takes Don's arm and pulls him round angrily*)

JULIE. Don't you dare lay a finger on him.
DON. The trouble with you is that you can't make up your mind. Five minutes ago you were urging me to knock his block off.
JULIE. That was quite different, he thought you were carrying me off to the bedroom.
SALLY (*horrified*) What's that, Don!
DON. It was an accident.
BILL. It looked pretty deliberate to me.
JULIE. A fine bloke *you* married. (*She plumps herself down at the* R *end of the settee*)

(SALLY *advances to her, furious*)

SALLY. Now you keep out of this.
BILL. Now steady on you two.
DON. I can explain everything, it was just a case of mistaken identity.
JULIE. Absolute rubbish, he shouldn't be at large, he's a menace.
SALLY. What did you call my husband?

(*Pandemonium breaks out as they all argue at the tops of their voices.*

In the middle of this, WOODY *walks in through the french windows. He is an inoffensive little man who carries a rod in a canvas bag and a tin of bait. He puts his case down and beams at them*)

WOODY (*cheerfully*) Good evening.

(*They all stop and stare at him*)

BILL. What's good about it?

WOODY (*doubtfully*) I appear to have made a small mistake. Could you tell me where *Chez Nous* is?

JULIE. This is it.

WOODY. Oh, well, I was right after all. Perhaps I'm too early.

(SALLY *crosses behind the settee and stares at him*)

SALLY. Who are you, anyway?

WOODY. Oh, let me introduce myself. My name is Woodburn and I've taken this cottage for the next two weeks.

SALLY. When?

WOODY. From today. I presume you are just leaving.

DON. You presume wrong.

WOODY. I don't understand.

BILL. Brother, you are not the only one. (*He crosses to the settee and sits beside Julie*)

WOODY. But I've got an agreement.

ALL. So have we.

WOODY. I don't think I've made a mistake. I specifically said the week commencing the twelfth, you see the competition starts on the fourteenth.

SALLY. What competition?

WOODY. The shallow water fishing from the pier. Would you mind holding this for a moment and I'll just check. (*He hands Sally the tin of bait*)

SALLY. Oooh, what an awful smell, what is it?

WOODY. Bait.

SALLY. Here, you take it, Don.

(DON *drifts down* R)

DON. Look, I've got enough trouble as it is.

WOODY (*producing an agreement*) Yes, here it is. "From noon the twelfth of August until noon the twenty-sixth. Eight guineas a week inclusive of bed linen and crockery." (*He puts it back in his pocket*)

BILL. There is something fishy here.

SALLY. Phew, you can say that again.

BILL. It looks to me as if we have all been sold a pup. Where did you see this place advertised?

WOODY. *The Angling Times.*
BILL. We got ours from *Dalton's Weekly.* Where did you get yours?
DON. I er ... I'd rather not say.
BILL. Well, we have got to know, come on.
DON. The—er, *Nursing Mirror.*
SALLY. You never told me that.
DON. You never asked me.
JULIE. We've obviously all been taken for a ride. What are we going to do?
WOODY. Well, I don't wish to appear selfish, but this is rather important to me. You see I have won the competition these last two years and if I win it again the cup will be mine.
JULIE. That's all very well, but we have only just got married.
WOODY. I appreciate that, but if I may say so, you are going to be married a lifetime—(*he looks at Don*) but the competition only lasts a week.
SALLY (*exploding*) Well, of all the selfish ideas that takes a lot of beating.
WOODY. No, not selfish, practical. Now where is the bedroom, please?
SALLY (*dazed*) Well, it's over there.
WOODY. Thank you. (*Leaving his bag on the floor he marches over to the door* L)

(BILL *gets up and bars his way*)

BILL. Over my dead body.

(SALLY *comes down behind Woody to hand him his bait.* BILL *gets hold of his rod and they both struggle with it. In desperation she turns to* DON *who won't take it either*)

WOODY (*heatedly*) Please, mind my rod, you'll damage it, let go.
BILL. Not until ...
WOODY. Will you let go? (*Angrily*) I'm warning you for the last time.

(SALLY *bends down to put the bait on the floor. There is a terrific struggle for the rod and* BILL *lets go.* WOODY *unprepared for this, swings round with the rod and catches Sally a resounding smack across the backside*)

SALLY. Oooh! You struck me.

(WOODY *drops the rod on the floor, terrified*)

DON. That's done it.

WOODY (*heatedly*) I assure you it was an accident. It was his fault, if this idiot had let go when I asked him to . . .

BILL. Did you call me an idiot?

JULIE (*springing up*) How dare you talk to my husband like that.

WOODY (*floundering*) Don't be so unreasonable. I'm trying to explain. If *she* hadn't been in the way . . .

DON. Oh, so now it's my wife's fault, is it?

WOODY. I didn't say that, all I meant was . . .

(*They all start talking at once.*
In the middle of this ZINA *enters at the french windows. She is a Bohemian type, wearing gay clothes and coloured stockings. All her gestures are greatly exaggerated. She puts her bag down and flings her arms out dramatically*)

ZINA (*gushing*) Darlings!

(*They all stop and stare at her, amazed*)

(*She comes down to them*) Darlings. You've beaten me to it, but how lovely to see you all. I thought I'd never find the place. Oh, this is going to be fun, isn't it. Now who do I share with? You? (*To Don*) You? (*To Bill*) Or you? (*She goes to point to Woody, but thinks better of it and ends up pointing at Bill again*)

JULIE (*coldly*) I beg your pardon.

ZINA (*unabashed*) Ooops, sorry, have you beaten me to the post?

SALLY. Look, I think I'm going mad in a minute. Let's sit down and find out what is going on.

BILL. Good idea.

(SALLY *sits* R *of the table,* DON *sits in the other chair.* JULIE *sits on the settee with* BILL *on her left.* WOODY *perches on the chair left of the settee*)

ZINA. But, darling, there is nothing *to* find out.

SALLY. But there must be. In the first place, what did you mean when you said we'd beaten you to it?

"THIS DESIRABLE COTTAGE . . ." 19

ZINA. What I said. You got here first. I didn't expect you all until tomorrow.

JULIE. But how can you expect us when you have never even seen us before?

ZINA. But, my sweet, I invited you all down here last week.

BILL (*dazed*) You did?

(ZINA *goes to the back of the settee and leans over to him*)

ZINA. But, of course, darling, at Bingo's party.

BILL. But I've never heard of Bingo.

DON. I thought it was a game.

(ZINA *trills with laughter and glides over to Don*)

ZINA. Oh, isn't he cute? Are you sure I didn't invite you?

DON. Positive.

(ZINA *stands there at* C, *trying to think*)

ZINA. Well, I know it was at the end of the party, but I wasn't that tiddly. Surely I couldn't have made a mistake. (*She notices Woody then points a long finger at him*) I recognize you, anyway.

WOODY (*uncomfortably*) Me?

ZINA. Yes, you do nudes in charcoal on the pavement in Sloane Square.

WOODY (*with dignity*) I assure you, madam, I've never done a nude in my life.

BILL. That doesn't surprise me.

ZINA (*happily*) Oh, well, then I've made a mistake. Who are you all then?

DON. This is Sally and I'm Don—(*miserably*) and we are supposed to be on our honeymoon.

(ZINA *leans towards him*)

ZINA. Oh, how sweetly old-fashioned. Never mind. (*She wafts over to Julie*) And you?

BILL. This is Julie and I'm Bill. We've just got married, too.

ZINA. Don't tell me you are on . . .

BILL (*glumly*) Yes.

ZINA (*pointing*) And who are you?

WOODY. My name is Woodburn.
ZINA (*happily*) How nice for you.
JULIE. What's your other name?
WOODY. Er—Sebastion. (*He pronounces it "Sebarstion"*)
ZINA. Oh, you poor man.
BILL. That lays yourself open a bit, doesn't it?
DON (*cheerfully*) Well, I know what we'll call *you* for short.
SALLY. Don!
WOODY. My friends call me—er, Woody.
DON (*in an affected voice*) They do? Jolly good.

(SALLY *slaps* DON *on the arm. He subsides*)

JULIE. After all this, who are you?
ZINA. I'm Zina.
JULIE. Zina what?
ZINA. Just Zina.
SALLY. Not Smith or Brown or anything?
ZINA. No. Annigoni is Annigoni, Sabrina is Sabrina and I'm Zina. I paint.
DON (*grinning*) What, nudes with violins and things?
ZINA. Sometimes.
DON. I've got a brilliant idea. (*He points to Woody*) What about, "Nude with a fishing-rod"?

(ZINA *slaps* DON *very heartily on the shoulder, he nearly collapses*)

ZINA. That's the sort of spirit we want. (*She sits happily on the floor*) I can see this is going to be a wonderful fortnight, and when the others come . . .
BILL. What others?
ZINA. The people I invited at Bingo's party.
BILL. How many?
ZINA. Oh, I don't know, the room was pretty full at the time, about a dozen I should say.
JULIE. A dozen! In this tiny place?
ZINA. Why not? The more the merrier.
JULIE (*wailing*) But this is my honeymoon.
ZINA. But, darling, what's a honeymoon? You can have that at any time.
JULIE (*stubbornly*) I want it now.
ZINA. Oh, don't be so selfish, you are spoiling the party.

"THIS DESIRABLE COTTAGE . . ." 21

(JULIE *gets to her feet angrily*)

JULIE (*exasperated*) Well, that's rich. I've heard everything now. Come on, Bill, we'll find rooms in the village.

WOODY. You won't, I'm afraid, everything is booked up, I tried months ago, there are over a hundred anglers down for the competition, some of them are sleeping five and six to a room.

ZINA (*getting up*) Well, if they can do it, so can we. Now which is the bedroom, this?

(ZINA *strides out* L. BILL *jumps up to try and stop her, but is too late, she has gone*)

BILL. Hey, now wait a minute. (*He goes behind the settee*) Look, something has got to be done about that woman, she's a menace.

SALLY (*weakly*) Right now I feel I couldn't care less what happens except (*she points at Woody*) to wake up and find that beside me on the pillow in the morning.

DON. Now don't take it out on poor Woody, it's not his fault.

JULIE. Well, whose fault is it—can somebody tell me that? (*She sits angrily on the settee again*)

WOODY. Mr Rosenberg who let the cottage to all of us at the same time.

BILL. When I lay my hands on that . . .

(ZINA *enters* L)

Hey, Zina, who did you get this cottage from?

ZINA. Benny Rosenberg.

BILL. Where does he live?

ZINA. The last time I saw him he was leaving rather quickly for Tel Aviv.

BILL. I thought as much, the crook.

ZINA. Oh, no, darling, Benny's a poppet.

DON. Well, apart from letting cottages four times over, what does he do for a living?

ZINA. He supplies models. (*She sits on the* L *arm of the settee with her feet on the seat*)

WOODY. Models? Oh, you mean trains.

ZINA. No, dear, models. You've seen the little postcards in the windows, haven't you? "Interesting model, thirty-four—twenty-three—thirty-six, ring Whitehall three-o-four-six any time"?

WOODY (*blankly*) No, I haven't.

ZINA. Oh, you *have* got a lot to catch up with, haven't you?

SALLY (*wearily*) Well, what's the plan?

ZINA. I've had a look at the room, it's tiny. That bed will hold three and no more.

SALLY. So?

ZINA. Well, we'll just have to get organized, that's all. This sofa will take two and someone else can make do with those two chairs. Now how shall we divide up. Who has got a pack of cards?

WOODY (*innocently*) I think I have a pack in my . . .

BILL (*quickly*) Oh, no, you don't. You stick to fishing.

ZINA. Of course, if you want to be conventional, all the girls can share the bedroom with the boys out here, but it's going to be an awfully dull party. I mean, what can three girls find to talk about all night?

JULIE. I want to sleep.

ZINA. Darling, you can sleep at any time, we shall be drinking until daylight. I've got bottles of it in my case.

JULIE. You can drink yourself to death for all I care, but I'm going to sleep.

ZINA. Oh, darling, don't be such a kill-joy.

SALLY (*miserably*) But what about Don?

ZINA. Well, what about him?

SALLY. It may be old-fashioned to you, but I happen to be on my honeymoon and I put it to you, who wants to spend a honeymoon with a girl?

BILL (*grimly*) *I* do.

WOODY (*suddenly*) I wonder which would be the coolest place to put my bait.

DON (*viciously; getting up*) Why don't you shove it . . .

SALLY. Don!

DON (*plumping down again*) Well, he did ask for it.

(JULIE *jumps to her feet and moves round to Bill behind the settee*)

JULIE (*furious*) This is an impossible situation. Bill, get our bags and we'll catch the first train out of here.

SALLY. Where are you going?

"THIS DESIRABLE COTTAGE . . ." 23

Julie. Anywhere, I don't care if it is Clapham Junction. Anything to get away from this. Go on, Bill.
Woody. You are wasting your time, I'm afraid. The train we came down on was the last one of the day.
Julie. Are you sure?
Woody. Positive, there isn't another one out until nine o'clock on Monday morning.
Julie. We'll have to take a taxi then.
Woody. That's no good either, I'm afraid. There is only one and it's broken down, I tried to get it to bring me here from the station.
Bill. Why don't you go and haunt some other cottage?
Woody. I was only trying to be helpful.
Julie. Well, it looks like a couple of nights on the sand-dunes.
Woody. Well, if you . . .
Julie. No, don't tell me, there is a storm warning.
Woody. Rain *is* forecast.
Julie (*furiously*) Oooh! This is all your fault, Bill—you and your promise of a quiet little country cottage miles from anywhere.
Don (*coming over to them*) Now don't take it out on Bill, he wasn't to know.
Julie. Well, he should have made sure.
Sally (*moving to Don*) And if it comes to that, *you* should have made sure, too. Now look at the mess you've both landed us in.
Bill } (*together*) { We've landed you in . . . etc.
Don } { Well, of all the . . . etc.
Julie. Neither of you seem to have the ability to organize a schoolgirls' outing.
Sally. I agree.
Don (*exasperated*) I paid my money and I've got a receipt for it, what more could I do?
Bill. Me, too.
Woody. I appear to be the only person with an actual agreement. (*He produces it again*)
Don (*furious*) If you bring that flaming thing out again, I'll . . .
Sally (*curtly*) There is no need to lose your temper with Sebastion, just because he happens to state his side of the argument.

JULIE. I agree.
BILL (*almost speechless*). What's all this sudden ganging up with Champion the Wonder Horse here?
SALLY. Ganging up?
BILL. Yes. Five minutes ago you were willing to tear him apart, and now when he opens his mouth it's a question of "let no dog bark".
SALLY. I think you are being very rude to Sebastion.
BILL (*to Don*) You see what I mean? It's Sebastion now. Please note, not Mr Woodburn, not Woody, but Sebastion. Well, if we are such a couple of skunks, you take him in there and we'll put up with Zina in here.

(ZINA *stands on the settee and faces Bill excitedly*)

ZINA. Darling, do you mean that?
BILL. Right now I'm so desperate I'd chance anything. (*He puts his hand on her shoulder and pushes her down viciously on to the seat*)
ZINA (*turning happily to Woody*) Well, that settles it very well. Go on, Sebastion, get your things in there.

(WOODY *gets to his feet, horrified*)

WOODY. What! Me in there with two girls?
ZINA. Well, that was the arrangement, wasn't it? What's bothering you?
WOODY (*desperately*) A joke is a joke, but there is a limit...
ZINA. But, darling, no-one is joking, splitting up like this will stop all this quarrelling, won't it?
WOODY. But I mean... Well, I mean to say...
ZINA. What are you getting so hot under the collar about? You said yourself that they were sleeping five and six to a room in the village, you are luckier than them, you've only got two.
WOODY. But they are all men.
ZINA. So what?
WOODY. Well, I can't go to bed with...
ZINA. But I keep telling you, no-one *is* going to bed, we are all going to have a party.

(JULIE *starts to laugh, she sits on the* R *arm of the settee then suddenly flops full length into it backwards, she laughs hysterically*)

SALLY. Julie! What's the matter, dear? Oh, gosh, she's

having hysterics. Well, don't just stand there, Bill, get some water.

BILL (*stupidly*) Water?—Oh, yes.

(BILL *rushes out* R *and reappears almost immediately with a little water in a cup. He rushes to the back of the settee and gently flicks drops into* JULIE'*s face. She still continues to laugh*)

DON (*harshly*) Here, give it to me, that's no good.

(DON *takes the cup from Bill, comes down to below the settee and flings the lot into* JULIE'*s face. She stops immediately. He hands the empty cup to Woody.* JULIE *sits up, furious*)

JULIE. Who did that? (*She sees Woody holding the empty cup and goes to him and gives him a hefty kick on the shins*) How dare you!

(WOODY *hops around holding his leg*)

WOODY. It wasn't me, it was him.

JULIE (*seeing Don*) You! (*She bends down quickly and seizes the fishing-rod*)

BILL (*yelling*) Duck, everyone!

(DON, *terrified, runs behind the table* R. *Everyone else ducks. Finding he is trapped* DON *bends down to escape the blow. She takes the rod above her head and brings it down with a tremendous bang on his back. The rod suddenly assumes a most peculiar shape as it breaks. There is an awful silence.* JULIE *turns to Woody*)

JULIE (*quietly*) Should—should it be like this?

WOODY (*agitated*) My rod! (*He goes over to her and takes it from her eyeing it in horror*) My prize-winning rod—look!

(*They all gaze at him*)

(*Suddenly he is transformed into a shouting sergeant-major. He issues orders left and right*) That's done it. It only needed this. Go on you girls, get your things into the bedroom. (*To Zina*) And *you*.

ZINA. But, darling . . .

WOODY. Don't you darling me. Jump to it!

ZINA. Isn't he wonderful?

(ZINA, SALLY and JULIE, *scared stiff, pile out of the room*, L)

WOODY. You two get some blankets from the girls and bring them out here. When you have done that, make up a rough bed on the settee. Go on, get a move on.

(BILL *and* DON *are galvanized into action and go out* L)

(*He wanders sadly to the kitchen door looking at his rod*) My beautiful rod, finished.

(BILL *and* DON *return from the bedroom with the blankets*)

(*He puts his rod against the wall then turns to them*) Where are the girls?

DON. In the bedroom—sir.

WOODY. Well, get them.

DON (*at the door* L) You are wanted. Quick.

(*They appear* L *and form a huddled queue headed by* SALLY, *then* JULIE, *with* ZINA *at the back. They face him apprehensively*)

WOODY (*coming* C) Now, which one of you can cook?

(*They hold a brief muttered council*)

SALLY (*timorously*) I can.

WOODY. Right. First thing in the morning, you get the breakfast.

SALLY. But we've nothing to make it with.

WOODY (*astounded*) Didn't any of you bring anything?

JULIE (*nervously*) Only a little tea.

WOODY (*sharply*) Speak up, girl.

JULIE (*shouting*) Only a little tea.

WOODY. And what did you bring?

(ZINA *peeps out coyly from behind the other two*)

ZINA. Just little me.

WOODY (*tartly*) Well, I can't say I fancy *you* for breakfast.

ZINA (*laughing to the others*) What a wonderful remark, did you hear . . . ? (*She suddenly notices his expression and cowers behind the others again*)

WOODY. Right then. The men will put ten bob into the kitty, that should see us through to Monday morning.

(BILL *and* DON *give him ten shillings each then go back to their places*)

(*He adds his own note then points at Julie*) You!
JULIE (*scared*) Me?
WOODY. Yes.

(ZINA *and* SALLY *push her forward. She approaches Woody nervously*)

(*He puts the money into her hand*) Now, first thing in the morning you get up, go to the nearest farm and buy some eggs, butter, milk and bread. When you have done that bring it back here and give it to her. (*He points to Sally*) Breakfast at half past seven.
ALL (*scandalized*) Half past seven!
WOODY (*firmly*) That's what I said. Any questions?

(*No-one answers*)

Right. Everyone get to bed now, I'm putting out the lights in five minutes. Well, don't just stand there, *move*.

(ZINA, SALLY *and* JULIE *bustle out* L, JULIE *turns back at the door*)

JULIE (*nervously*) Would it be all right if we just popped in to kiss our husbands good night?
WOODY. If you are not too long about it.
JULIE (*gratefully*) Oh, thank you.

(JULIE *goes out* L *after the others*)

WOODY. Well, that seems to have settled everything. You two had better make up a bed on the settee and I'll take these two chairs. Now this is the kitchen, I suppose?
BILL. Yes.
WOODY. I'll put my things in there.

(WOODY *picks up his suitcase from the window and goes out* R)

BILL (*quietly*) I wouldn't have believed it.
DON. Nor me.
BILL. Why are we doing all this?
DON. I don't know.
BILL. Well, give him his due, he's organized the girls.

(WOODY *enters again, he comes* C)

WOODY. There doesn't seem to be a . . .

Don. The little shed at the bottom of the garden.
Woody. Oh, thank you.

(Woody *strides out through the window*)

Bill. I ask you, Don, where does a fieldmouse like that suddenly get all this authority?
Don. Probably a shop steward in the fisherman's union. Now what's the best way to fix this bed?

(*The bedroom door L opens and* Zina *pokes her head out*)

Zina. Psst! Is the coast clear?
Bill. Yes, he's in the garden.
Zina. I just wanted my case, it's got all the liquor in it. (*She crosses* C *then turns to them*) Did you ever see such a man?
Don. Frankly, no.
Zina. But he's wasted, he ought to be head of NATO or something.
Bill. How are the girls?
Zina. Pretty shaken at the moment, they are even talking in whispers. Look, we are doing it, too. This is ridiculous.
Bill (*sitting on the* L *arm of the settee*) I agree, after all we've all paid to be here.
Don. That's true, all the same we couldn't have arranged things any other way though, could we?
Bill. That's not the point, Don, it's *our* honeymoon and we should be allowed to do our own organizing.
Zina. I agree. What about organizing a wildcat strike?
Bill. Who is going to be the leader?
Zina. Why, Don, of course.

(Don *sits firmly on the settee*)

Don. Not on your nelly, I've got enough trouble as it is.
Zina. But we must have a leader.
Don. What about you?
Zina (*quickly*) No, thank you.
Don. What, are you scared of him?
Zina. Me? Scared of *that*? Don, you are not serious?

(*A cough is heard from the garden*)

Bill. Look out, here he comes.

(Zina *grabs her case and quickly hides behind the* R *curtain of the window. The boys stand up.*

"THIS DESIRABLE COTTAGE . . ." 29

Woody *enters and comes down a little*)

Woody. Well, you haven't got on very fast, have you?
Don (*spreading a blanket quickly*) Oh, we were just about to start.
Woody. Your wife, does she cook a decent breakfast?
Don. I don't know, we've never had breakfast together yet.
Woody. Yes—yes, I see your point.

(Zina *giggles from behind the curtain.* Woody *strides to it and pulls it aside*)

Zina (*lamely*) Hullo.
Woody. What are you doing hiding there?
Zina. I was just collecting my night things. Night . . .

(Zina *scuttles out* L)

Woody. Well, one thing is certain, *she'll* have to go first thing Monday morning.

(Woody *strides out* R, *but stops to look at the boys who are suddenly galvanized into action. When he has gone they stop again*)

Bill. Which end do you want?
Don. I'm not fussy. Do you snore?
Bill. I don't know, I've never bothered to listen.

(*They take off their coats*)

It's not worth while undressing, is it?
Don. No, I suppose not.
Bill (*sitting gloomily on the settee*) Funny, you know, I never thought I'd be spending the first night of my honeymoon with you.
Don (*sitting beside him*) If it comes to that, you are not my idea of Brigitte Bardot either.
Bill. How can you think of Brigitte Bardot at a time like this?
Don. Easy, I can think of her at any time.
Bill (*indicating the kitchen*) I wonder what *he* thinks about?
Don. Fishing.
Bill. He's welcome.

(*There is a pause*)

Don. Bill?
Bill. Yes?
Don. Do you reckon we did the right thing getting married?

(BILL *just looks at him*)

I don't know either.

(*The door* L *opens and* SALLY *and* JULIE, *in their nighties, appear*)

SALLY (*whispering*) We've come to kiss you good night.
Don. O.K., the coast is clear.

(*The girls come across and settle on their husband's knees back to back. They all lie back comfortably in one cramped mass*)

JULIE. Oh, Bill, I'm sorry I behaved so badly.
BILL. Oh, that's all right, darling, it's been rather an unusual evening from the start.
SALLY. Have you forgiven me for being so nasty, Don?
Don. There is nothing to forgive.

(*They all kiss*)

SALLY. This is a bit of an anticlimax, isn't it?
Don. Yes.
JULIE. We didn't plan it this way, either.
SALLY. Oh, well, there is one consolation, nothing else could happen now.

(FRED *suddenly walks in briskly through the windows. He is foreman of a construction gang, has a large walrus moustache and wears dirty overalls with a cloth cap*)

FRED (*breezily*) 'Ullo, 'ullo, 'ullo, what's going on 'ere?

(*They all jump up and form a line facing him as he stands there in the middle of the room*)

JULIE. Oh, no, don't tell me you are staying here, too?
FRED. What are you talking about? I work here.
BILL. Then you haven't come to stay at this cottage?
FRED. Here! It's the last place I want to be right now.
SALLY. Oh, how wonderful, did you hear that?
FRED. What are you all doing here, anyway?
Don. We are on our honeymoon.

FRED. Well, that's a fine how do you do. You'll have to move I'm afraid.
DON. But we've only just arrived.
FRED. Can't help that, orders is orders.

(ZINA *enters* L *waving a bottle*)

ZINA. Yippee, the bar is open.
JULIE. Be quiet, we've got another crisis. (*To Fred*) What orders?
FRED. Didn't you know? This place is due for demolition.
BILL. What!
FRED. That's right, there's me orders in black and white. (*He takes them from his breast pocket*)
SALLY (*wailing*) But you can't, this is our honeymoon.
FRED. Sorry about that, miss, but you can't halt progress, you know.
DON. Now let's get this straight. Why has this cottage got to come down?
FRED. Because this comes in the extension to the airport runway. This adds another thousand yards to it, but you mark my words, when it's all finished they'll change their mind and start a helicopter service. (*He laughs at his own joke*)

(*They all stare*)

(*He stops abruptly*) Sorry. My little joke.
BILL. But you can't work in the middle of the night.
FRED. What do you mean, can't? We are on piecework, we never stop. I've got four bulldozers and twenty husky blokes out there just waiting for me to blow me whistle.
ZINA. Oh, how wonderful, bring them in and I'll open some more bottles.
JULIE (*wailing*) But you can't do this to us.
FRED. Can't I, you just watch.
JULIE. But this is my honeymoon night.
FRED. Doesn't look as if it's doing you much good, does it?
BILL. Don't you talk to my wife like that.
FRED. Sorry, no offence, I'm sure. All right then, now you all understand, you've got about five minutes to get clear before we start.
SALLY (*firmly*) I'm not moving from here.

JULIE. Nor me.
FRED. Well, that's up to you, miss, but when I blows me whistle, them bulldozers will come crashing in here and the whole place will collapse in an 'orrible heap of dust and rubble.
BILL. But that's murder.
FRED. It's orders.
DON. You can't do this to us.
ZINA. Do you know, I believe he's going to.
FRED. Now you've all had fair warning. When I blows me whistle . . .
DON (*testily*) Oh, shut up about your whistle.
FRED. Now then, that's no way to talk to a bloke . . .
DON. I'll talk to you as I damn well please.
SALLY. That's right, Don, you tell him.
FRED. Now look here . . .

(*There is a tremendous hubbub as they all shout FRED down.
In the middle of all this* WOODY *suddenly appears* R, *clad in a striped nightshirt*)

WOODY (*sternly*) What is the meaning of all this noise?

No-one takes any notice and they all hustle after FRED *who disappears quickly through the french windows blowing his whistle vigorously.* WOODY *wanders up to the windows, puzzled as—*

the CURTAIN *falls*

PRODUCTION NOTES

This play, prior to publication, has had about twenty performances, all of which have been hilariously received by large audiences.

It must, however, be played with tremendous speed and attack all the way through or it will sag badly.

Note that both girls, although their hats and gloves, etc., are different, both wear *identical* dresses.

The rod is quite simple to make. Take about five daily papers and roll them into a stiff roll about four and a half feet long. Insert this into a canvas rod case and you will have a rigid effect for normal handling. It will crumble very easily, however, when Don is beaten over the back with it, without hurting him. It does, in fact, go into almost frightening shapes and has been the cause of some of the biggest laughs in the play.

FURNITURE AND PROPERTY LIST

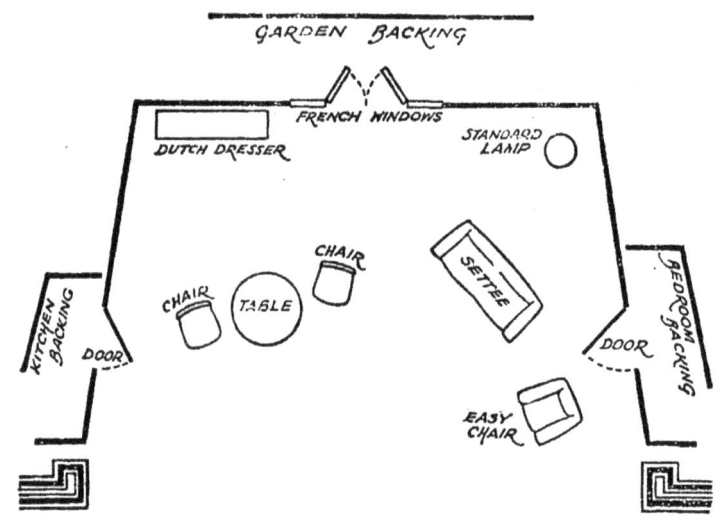

On stage: Small table
2 wheel-back chairs
Settee. *On it:* cushions
Easy chair
Dutch dresser. *On it:* cups, plates, etc., for dressing only
Curtains for the french windows

Off stage: 2 bags, picnic bag. *In it:* small bottle of milk, large piece of wood, agreement, cup of water, a blanket (BILL)
Case, agreement, blanket (DON)
Case, 2 cups, large wooden spoon (SALLY)
Fishing-rod in a case, bait in a tin, bag, agreement (WOODY)
Bag (ZINA)
A note of authority, whistle (FRED)

"THIS DESIRABLE COTTAGE . . ."

Personal: BILL: hat with confetti inside it, ten-shilling note
DON: ten-shilling note
WOODY: ten-shilling note
JULIA: wedding ring
SALLY: gloves, wedding ring
(JULIE and SALLY have identical dresses)

LIGHTING PLOT

Property fittings required: none
    Interior. The same scene throughout
    THE MAIN ACTING AREAS are RC, C and LC

To open: Effect of evening light outside the french windows
No cues

EFFECTS PLOT

Cue 1   BILL (*laughing*) "Oh, tripe."   (Page 11)
        Sound of heavy object being dropped in the bedroom

www.ingramcontent.com/pod-product-compliance
Ingram Content Group UK Ltd
Pitfield, Milton Keynes, MK11 3LW, UK
UKHW021848210426
5322IPUK00022B/543